T0381075

MAINTAINING
My Goodbye Party
Plans

Review YEARLY on:

- ❑ My Birthday
- ❑ New Year's Day
- ❑ Easter
- ❑ During Lent
- ❑ Memorial Day
- ❑ At the first funeral of the year
- ❑ On Retreat: scheduled for

_____
(date)

- ❑ Tax Day: April 15 or

_____

- ❑ Other:

_____

Review and Update every
FIVE YEARS
Next full update due in
_____ of 20___
(month)

The Goodbye Party

Workbook

Kim C. Rice

Order this book online at www.trafford.com
or email orders@trafford.com

Most Trafford titles are also available at major online book retailers.

Print information available on the last page.

ISBN: 978-1-4120-3594-1 (sc)

Trafford rev. 11/07/2018

Trafford
PUBLISHING®   www.trafford.com   &
North America & international
toll-free: 1 888 232 4444 (USA & Canada)
fax: 812 355 4082

Contents

Introduction

Hello and welcome! Planning for any goodbye is not usually easy or fun; in fact, with so many things to do and so many emotions racing around in us, planning can be physically and emotionally draining. Funeral planning is no different. And if the service has *not* been preplanned, decisions will need to be made quickly and often by those *without* the physical or emotional energy to make them thoughtfully. The goal of this workbook is to help make the overwhelming process of planning a funeral, your goodbye party, manageable.

As you begin this process, I encourage you to reshape how you think about funeral preplanning and even death. Many people think that this is a morbid thing to do and should be avoided. I disagree. Is it considerate for a person to plan a goodbye party when they know they will be leaving town? Do you think a funeral can be a goodbye party? Read the following story and think about what it says to you about funeral preplanning and death.

Imagine that you are going on a trip; it is a trip unlike any that you will ever take. Here is how it comes to be.

Long ago you were introduced to a man who had traveled the world. He was an intriguing man with many wonderful stories. You quickly became best friends. As he described his travels and all the places that he had visited, there was one place that captivated your imagination more than all the rest: a place so full of good people and beauty and glory that your desire to see it for yourself someday grew strong.

Then one day your friend told you that it was his time to return to the place that had intrigued you so, to his homeland. You asked if you could join him, but the answer was "No, not yet." After his departure, you exchanged letters and phone calls; and with each correspondence your longing grew to make this trip yourself and be with your friend once again.

Finally the day comes when you receive the good news: your friend tells you that his family will invite you to come to his home! Your invitation will be mailed to you, and once you receive it, you must get on the very next plane and begin your journey. What joy fills your heart! You begin to pack your bags!

Then you read the rest of the instructions that tell you more about this invitation. You must journey alone. You will not be able to return to the place you live now; this is a permanent move. And, you do not know when the invitation will arrive. It might arrive tonight, tomorrow, or in the next five, six or fifty-six years! The surprising, and somewhat disturbing, fact is you do not know when you will be called to leave.

You feel torn. You want to go on this trip. But you do not want to leave your home and your family and friends behind. And you would like a little more notice about when you are going to be invited. Pondering this dilemma, you realize that you have a decision to make. You can choose to "forget" that the invitation is coming and go about your life "as normal." Or you can choose to live in the tension of living life fully, while being prepared to leave at a moment's notice. If you elect the second option, you will still need to begin packing your bags now. And you will be wise to prepare your life so that when you leave, your loved ones are taken care of, your "house is in order" and there is closure for your relationships. One thoughtful way to live in this tension is to begin planning and talking about your goodbye party now.

Do you see the relationship between the story and funeral preplanning? The fact is that we are all going to die, and not one of us knows the date or time of our death. Some of us will choose to do some preplanning. But most of us will choose to "forget" that we are going to die someday. We refuse to make any plans that remind us of this fact. So when we do die, our family and friends are left to plan our funeral, our goodbye party, *while* experiencing grief and shock.

I encourage you to give yourself permission to plan your funeral, your goodbye party, now. You are going to die. We are all going to die. As a gift to yourself and to your loved ones, read on and do as much of the preplanning as you can. Think of it as packing your bags and making your travel plans!

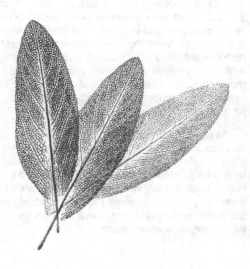

How To Use This Workbook

The goal of this workbook is to make the process of preplanning a funeral manageable and less imposing. There are many creative ways to make this work more enjoyable and meaningful, such as doing the work with other people, breaking it down into manageable steps and so forth. On the following page, I suggest possible methods to help you begin and complete the task. One recommendation that I urge you to follow is to make the task as enjoyable as you can: go to a coffee shop or restaurant, have dessert and your favorite beverage, talk and laugh while working. This task does not have to be difficult. I encourage you to think "outside the box" both in the planning of your funeral and in your method of planning. Remember the story from the Introduction; keep that story in mind as you plan and prepare for your funeral, your goodbye party!

I recommend that you read the book, *The Goodbye Party*[1], in order to gain the overall picture of preplanning your funeral, and for detailed information and the rationale for each form. The next workbook section, **Notes From the Author: About Specific Forms**, covers only the essentials on select forms that warrant specific instruction.

Recommendations for completing this workbook:

1. Look through the forms to get a general feel for the scope of the task. As you go, make notes about the things that you already have an opinion on. If you are unsure of your preferences, it can be helpful to state what you know you do not want. Use pencil throughout the workbook; that way changes through the years are easy to make.

2. Fill out page xix: **My Thoughts and Goals for Planning My Goodbye Party**. Set a goal date for completion of the workbook.

3. Decide on a method that will best help you complete the workbook by the date you have set as your goal. On the following page are some method options. (Feel free to adapt these methods to meet your needs, or create your own method. It is important that the method you choose works for you.)

Method Options

A. Complete the workbook in one to three sittings. Complete the A forms one day, B forms next, and C forms last. If this method appeals to you, going on one to three retreats for the specific purpose of completing this workbook may be beneficial.

B. Complete the forms that interest you first, and then complete the forms that are left. You may want to take the forms out of the workbook and divide them into three piles: most interesting, moderately interesting, and not so interesting. Complete one pile per month, per quarter or per year!

C. Complete your funeral plans within a twelve month time period by using the calendar pages that are arranged in this workbook.

   ❏ Decide when you will start. Write the month and year that you are beginning on page 3 (First Month), and fill in the date boxes; do this for all twelve months. Use the calendar to indicate which days of the month you plan to set aside time to work on your plans. There is a sample calendar on page 1.

   ❏ Leave the workbook out where you can see it often for these next twelve months (yet also choose a place that affords privacy). You may wish to leave the calendar page open to the current month that you are working on, so you can add ideas and work on these forms in small sections throughout the month.

   ❏ Work on the sections arranged for each month. If you have extra time and energy one month, you may want to work ahead on a section of interest.

D. Complete the workbook in community. Your plans may gain more meaning and depth if you share them and talk about the feelings you have as you prepare for your death. Choose a person or group that you trust and want to share this time with. Here are two methods for completing the workbook in community.

   ❏ Ask your spouse, a friend or family member to help you. Choose Method A, B or C. Your helper may ask you the questions on the forms and write your answers down for you, or you may each fill out your own forms while in each other's company. Make it enjoyable and meaningful. Go out for dinner or coffee. Have dessert!

   ❏ Gather a group of friends together: meet monthly or for a weekend retreat. Complete the forms individually, and share your thoughts, questions, ideas and opinions when you gather. Or meet and work on "the form of the month" for an hour and then have a discussion about the current form and the form for next month. One person, or perhaps all group members, may bring a song or symbol that they want in their funeral each time you gather. Make the gatherings fun and include time to socialize.

Remember, no matter which method you choose, to make your planning times as pleasant as you can. Go to a coffee shop, go out for dinner, or have dessert and your favorite beverage. Get comfortable and start writing!

Notes from the Author

About Preparing Your Goodbye Party

1. Timing

Do an internal check to see if this is the right time for you to begin preparing your goodbye party. Are you currently feeling suicidal, depressed, intense anger, or manic? If you answered yes, this is likely not the time to work on this workbook. Seek professional help. Come back to this work when your mood is stable.

2. Definition of terms as I use them

Funeral	A service of remembrance for one who has died. I use this term whether the body is present or not. I use "goodbye party", "memorial service" and "funeral service" interchangeably.
Wake	The informal time before a funeral service, usually the night before and/or the day of the service. Friends and family are able to gather to support those separated from the one who died. "Vigil" or "visitation" are other terms commonly used to describe this time.
Bedside Vigil	The time before death, when death is near. This can occur at any location: in a hospital, a hospice, at home, a nursing home or many other locations.
Committal Service	The time at the grave when burial occurs. This can also be the time when the ashes are placed or scattered. I use "grave-side service" and "committal service" interchangeably. Another term for this time is "interment".
Meal of Consolation	The meal that usually follows the funeral or memorial service, either before or after the committal service. The term "meal of consolation" comes from the Jewish tradition. It speaks to a deeper purpose for this meal than just to feed the bodies of those grieving. A full explanation of the meal of consolation can be found in the book, *The Goodbye Party*.

3. **Repetition**

   You will find that many forms ask for the same or related information. This allows you to work on any form in any order. If you do not wish to repeat the information, just note that you have filled it in on another form.

4. **Time Frame**

   You may wonder how to fill out the forms, knowing that you may not die for a long time. I suggest that you fill out the forms based on your preferences and life *today*. Things will change, of course, and therefore I strongly suggest you review these plans yearly and thoroughly revise them every five years.

5. **Division of Forms**

   I have divided the nineteen forms into three sections; A, B and C. This division is based on my thoughts about what is most important in funeral planning. If you were to ask other experts, they might suggest other groupings for the forms. There is no right or wrong way to do this. Here is my rationale for grouping the forms the way I did: I have divided the forms into these sections for the sole purpose of making it easier to prioritize, especially if you choose method A (from page x). The "A" forms are more likely to help your family immediately, even before death. The "B" forms are also helpful, containing information that your family and friends will not likely know. The "C" forms contain many details and are certainly helpful as well, but may not be as helpful if they are the only forms completed. Reprioritize the forms if a different order makes more sense to you. Think about what would help you most if a family member died today. Consider what information will help your family and friends when you die.

6. **Notes**

   I have provided pages for notes at the back of the workbook. Please use these pages to write down thoughts, ideas and opinions that do not seem to fit onto a worksheet yet. This is the place to put your thoughts before you are sure of them. It is also a place where you can attach items that may be examples of what you like or dislike, such as obituaries, funeral programs, verses, poems and so forth. I encourage you to draw on these pages; you may wish to draw about death, where you believe you will be when you die, or just sketch randomly.

7. **Storage**

   I recommend that you purchase a portable file folder or a strong, zippered three-ring binder to keep your completed workbook and other important documents that will be needed when you die or are close to death. Important documents include a Health Care Power of Attorney, will, title to house and vehicles, and so forth. Keep originals in your safe deposit box and copies in this binder. I encourage you to put copies of favorite songs into this folder. This can be a place to store scraps of ideas until you are ready to put them onto your workbook forms. As soon as you purchase a file or binder, mark the **My Thoughts and Goals for Planning My Goodbye Party** page, to indicate that you have such a storage container. The person who plans the final details will appreciate that everything is in one place and is portable. Portability also makes it easier for you to take your plans on retreat or to a coffee shop; anything you can do to make this job easier and pleasant will help you prepare and keep at it.

8. **Faith**

No matter what your faith beliefs or traditions are, this workbook is intended for you. Many of these forms ask for or suggest faith-related thoughts and feelings. Scripture is placed throughout the workbook. I give you permission to cross out any question or quote and replace it with a thought that makes more sense to you. I refer you to the chapter entitled "Goodbye, Hello: Every Exit is an Entrance" in the book, *The Goodbye Party,* that addresses faith issues related to death.

9. **Final Preplanning Tasks**

There are some tasks associated with preplanning your funeral that do not fit onto a form or worksheet. I have left room on each calendar page for you to add any of these tasks. Another option would be to complete these tasks during the thirteenth month, after all of your other planning is completed. The tasks that complete the planning process are:

- ❏ Meet with the person(s) who you would like to officiate at your goodbye party service. Give this person a copy of your plans and inform him/her of the location of your plans.

- ❏ Meet with the person(s) you have assigned as "Designated Person to help with final details", page xix. Give this person a copy of your plans and inform him/her of the location of your plans.

- ❏ Visit and interview the cemetery(s) you are considering. I suggest that you visit more than one.

- ❏ Visit and interview the funeral home you are considering. Visit more than one.

- ❏ Begin prepaying for the property at the cemetery.

- ❏ Begin prepaying all of your funeral expenses at the funeral home.

- ❏ Purchase an urn or casket.

- ❏ Purchase a register book (guest book) for your service.

10. **In General**

I have tried to make these forms as self-explanatory as I can. Remember that if you do not do this work and write down your preferences, someone will have to do it. They will have to do it in the midst of intense grief and in just one to three days. You, most likely, have the luxury of planning your goodbye party over the next several years. Please do it! Then maintain it! Look at these forms every year (perhaps at Easter, your birthday, New Year's Day, or while on retreat); and then make sure to revise them every five years, because things will change. These are working documents, so use pencil and record the date when you update them. Keep them in a safe place, and let your family and friends know where they are kept. As Sara Groves, singer and songwriter, says, "You are never too young to think about it."[2]

About Specific Forms

Below are explanations to help you fill out the most complicated forms. I refer you to the book, *The Goodbye Party*, in order to see the entire picture of funeral planning and for specifics and the rationale for each form in this workbook.

1. **A-3: About Me.** The purpose of this form is to provide basic information about you that will be needed to complete the death certificate, the obituary and the eulogy. The section on passwords and information for death certificates may be lacking from any other information your family can find easily. Make sure to complete this form!

2. **A-4: Health Care Power of Attorney (HCPA) Example.** This is exactly that—an example of a HCPA and nothing else. Please make sure to check the legal requirements for the state in which you live to ensure that the HCPA you create is legal. This example of a HCPA also serves as a health care advance directive (or living will). A quick definition of the difference between a Health Care Advance Directive/living will and a HCPA: a) a Health Care Advance Directive/living will are usually not legal documents and they are generally used only close to death, b) a HCPA is a legal document that gives power to the person that you appoint to legally make medical decisions for you if you are unable to speak for yourself and need care. I highly recommend that you have a HCPA in place, even if you are young and healthy, even if you are married. In many states your spouse is not legally entitled to make medical decisions for you unless you designate him or her as your HCPA. Please consult an attorney and the law in your state for further information. And remember, the information contained in these documents, both individually and collectively, should not be considered legal advice. Before taking advantage of any of these documents for legal use, an individual is encouraged to consult with a knowledgeable attorney.

3. **B-2: Funeral To Do List.** I have listed most of the items that I know may need to be decided or acted upon within the first three days of death and up to a year after death. Many of these immediate tasks can be carried out by the funeral home. If you prepay for your funeral, clarify which of these items will be the responsibility of your funeral director and which will be your family's responsibility. As you look at the To Do List, cross out any items that will not apply to your funeral. Add any items that I have not included. You may want to note why you crossed something off to avoid confusion by those planning the final details.

4. **B-3: Care Calendar.** This form provides a way for you to encourage and comfort those most dear to you after you have died. During a time of intense grief, most people find it difficult to care for themselves. The purpose of this form is to give your loved one(s) a gift of your words and help when you are not able to be with them in person. Consider what that person will need to know and do when you are no longer with them. Write three to four items in each of the thirty-five boxes. You might include comfort foods to eat, people to spend time with, chores to do (such as laundry) and so on. Also include reminders from you about special memories that are dear to your heart. You know your loved one(s) best. What will they have a hard time doing when you are gone? What will they need to know about your thoughts and memories about them?

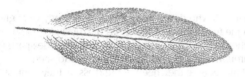

If you are a parent, with young or grown children, you may wish to make a Care Calendar for each of your children and grandchildren and a separate Care Calendar for your spouse. Perhaps you are single, or in a troubled marriage; consider the pros and cons of completing a Care Calendar. I encourage you to thoughtfully consider who to create Care Calendars for. Three copies are included in the workbook; make copies if you need more. Individualize each form for your spouse, close friend(s), child(ren), grandchild(ren), parent(s), or other important people in your life.

Each Care Calendar has a place to designate an "accountability person." Indicate a friend or relative who will be able to walk alongside your loved one for at least the first thirty-five days after your death. This is the person who will be able to ask your loved one how they are doing and if they are following the Care Calendar plans.

5. **Funeral Service: B-6: The Funeral Service, B-7: The Committal Service, C-5: Obituary, Eulogy and Grave Marker, C-6: Order of Service, C-7: My Funeral Program.** These forms contain specific information about the Funeral Service itself. Some faith communities and traditions may not allow you to add all that is present in these forms, such as your own eulogy. I advise you to meet with a representative from your faith community to share your desires about your funeral. This will be a time when you can find out if some part of your plan needs to be adjusted. Elements of your plans that do not fit into a liturgical service can be carried out at a different time such as at the wake or committal service.

6. **About Death Certificates.** Death certificates are mentioned on forms **A-3: About Me,** and **B-2: Funeral To Do List.** In addition to filling in the information, you will need to estimate how many death certificates your family will need. I recommend basing this estimate (as I recommend for all of the planning) on how many would be needed if you were to die today. Your family will need one death certificate for each piece of property that is in your name (i.e. house, car, boat, stocks, bank CDs) and for any place that you have a debt (i.e. credit cards, bank loans, student loans). Regarding stocks, your family will need a death certificate for each stock held, not just for the brokerage house that holds many stocks for you. Use the section on **A-3: About Me** to figure out how many death certificates your family will need. It is common for many survivors to use ten to fifteen death certificates to settle the estate. Most businesses will require a certified copy of the death certificate and will not return it. By figuring out how many death certificates your family may need, you will save them extra steps and money at the time of your death.

7. **Candles/Roses to the Cross. C-6: Order of Service** and **C-7: My Funeral Program** reference times in the funeral service for "Candles/Roses to the Cross."
A goodbye party benefits from providing a time when those present can reconcile their differences; a time to acknowledge that none of us are perfect and that we have hurt each other, intentionally and unintentionally. Depending on your faith beliefs or traditions, this time can symbolize a bringing of sins and disappointments, done to and received from the deceased, to God for cleansing, reconciliation and release.

There are many ways to incorporate such a time into your funeral plans. One method might look like this: Give each person a candle or rose (or some other meaningful symbol) when they enter the service area. In the middle of the service have someone teach about the good that can come from reconciliation and release.

Invite all who desire to bring the object they were given to the front where a large cross or crucifix (or some other symbol of your faith) is located. Provide space through music or silence for the guests to spend whatever time they need at the cross as they confess the ways that they have sinned against the deceased, as well as to acknowledge the ways that the deceased sinned against them. The candles or roses can be left at the cross as a symbol of release. I encourage you to find some way to incorporate a time into your goodbye party to acknowledge that you did hurt others here on earth and may not have had time to reconcile each hurt.

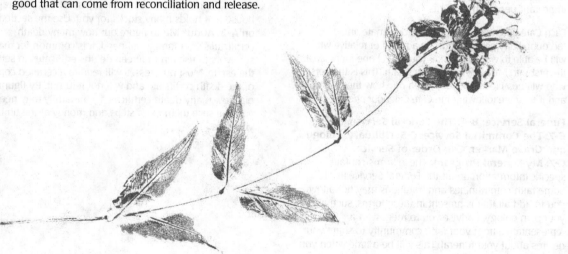

To the Person Designated to Follow the Plans of the One Who Has Died

1. **A2: People to Notify** and **B2: Funeral To Do List** will help you as you begin the process of facilitating the funeral for your family member or friend.

2. Look at the workbook **Contents** to find out where the information you will need is located. Copy any forms needed. Keep the original forms in a safe place so that they are available for reference if the copies are lost. Give a copy of the completed forms to the person who will lead the funeral service and a copy to the funeral home director, if needed.

3. Make sure to check **Notes** for other information that your loved one may have left for you.

4. There may be a portable file folder or zippered binder that your loved one used to store funeral-related items (such as a will, title to house and vehicles, music for the funeral service and other items).

   Look for the location of this file in

   this room:_____

   of address:_____,

   description of file is:_____

   _____
   *(if the location is not written here, check **My Thoughts and Goals for Planning My Goodbye Party**).*

5. If your loved one did not complete all of the forms, you may still find this workbook helpful. First, copy all forms that you may need. Use the uncompleted forms to gather information from other family and friends. Delegate responsibilities among family and friends by giving a copy of one or more forms to each person willing to help with some detail of the planning.

6. Most likely you will not be able to follow the plans written in this workbook exactly. They are meant to guide you. Do your best to follow them, but also do what is best for those alive now.

7. Use this space for questions or notes to yourself. May you find the strength, courage and peace that you need to do this work.

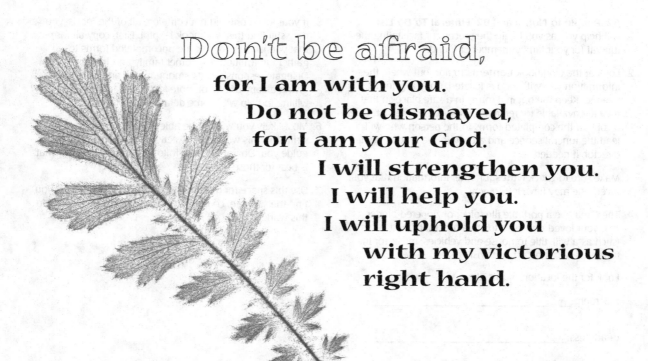

Don't be afraid,

for I am with you.
Do not be dismayed,
for I am your God.
I will strengthen you.
I will help you.
I will uphold you
with my victorious
right hand.

Isaiah 41:10 (NLT)

My Thoughts and Goals for Planning My Goodbye Party

My Full and Legal Name

_____

Date begun_____

Goal date for completion of these funeral planning forms

_____

_____

Reasons that I want to plan my funeral

_____

_____

_____

Other thoughts and questions

_____

_____

_____

Other goals related to funeral planning

_____

_____

My goal for maintaining my funeral plans

_____

_____

Complete in pencil:

Designated person to help with the final details of my funeral

Name _____

Phone _____

Other phone _____

Alternate contact person *(if first person is unavailable)*
Name _____

Phone _____

Other phone _____

Comments and other important information

_____

_____

_____

❏ I have a file/binder that contains all or most of the necessary information to supplement the information in this workbook.

The file is located in this room _____

of address _____

description of file is_____

_____

O God of endings,

you promised to be with me always,
even to the end of time.
Move with me now in these occasions of last things,
of shivering vulnerabilities and letting go:
letting go of parents gone, past gone, friends going, old self growing;
letting go of children grown, needs outgrown,
prejudices ingrown, illusions overgrown;
letting go of swollen grudges and shrunken loves.

Be with me in my end of things,
my letting go of dead things, dead ways, dead words,
dead self I hold so tightly, defend so blindly, fear losing so frantically.

I teeter on the brink of endings:
some anticipated, some resisted, some inevitable, some surprising,
most painful; and the mystery of them quiets me to awe.

In silence, Lord, I feel now the curious blend of grief
and gladness in me over the endings
that the ticking and whirling of things brings;
and I listen for your leading to help me
faithfully move on through the fear
of my time to let go so the timeless may take hold of me.

Ted Loder [3]

Sample Month

Month _____ July _____   Year _____ 2005 _____

Sunday	Monday	Tuesday	Wednesday	Thursday	Friday	Saturday
		1	2 Scan through workbook.	3	4	5
6	7	8	9	10	11	12
13	14 Begin workbook A-1	15	16	17	18	19
20	21	22	23	24	25	26
27	28	29	30	31 Finish A-1		

☑ **A-1: Bedside Vigil**

☐ _Call a cemetery_

☐ _____

☐ _____

☐ _____

☐ _____

How do you know what will happen tomorrow?

For your life is like the morning fog—
it's here a little while, then it's gone.

James 4:14 (NLT)

Come now, you who say, "Today or tomorrow we will go to such and such a city, and spend a year there and engage in business and make a profit." Yet you do not know what your life will be like tomorrow. You are just a vapor that appears for a little while and then vanishes away. Instead, you ought to say, "If the Lord wills, we will live and also do this or that."

James 4:13–15 (NASB)

And now I have a word for you who brashly announce, "Today—at the latest, tomorrow—we're off to such and such a city for the year. We're going to start a business and make a lot of money." You don't know the first thing about tomorrow. You're nothing but a wisp of fog, catching a brief bit of sun before disappearing. Instead, make it a habit to say, "If the Master wills it and we're still alive, we'll do this or that."

James 4:13–15 (MSG)

First Month

Month _____   Year _____

Sunday	Monday	Tuesday	Wednesday	Thursday	Friday	Saturday

☐ **A-1: Bedside Vigil**

☐ _____
_____

☐ _____

☐ _____

☐ _____
_____

A-1: Bedside Vigil

Updated on_____

Circle what you desire, cross out what you do not desire, leave untouched those that are neutral.

	Please do…	Please do not…	Thoughts and Reasons	Other
Physical Touch				
❏ head rub ❏ hair combed				
❏ hand massage ❏ foot massage				
❏ spouse to lie in bed with me				
❏ other				
Comfort				
❏ special blanket wrapped around me				
❏ hand held ❏ other				
Scents				
❏ incense (if able) ❏ lotion (favorite scent)				
❏ candles (if able) ❏ perfume				
❏ flowers ❏ other				
Prayers				
❏ by one person ❏ by all				
❏ written ❏ spontaneous				
❏ constant, aloud ❏ constant, in silence				
❏ constant, mixture				
❏ scripture reading ❏ other				

Updated on _____

	Please do…	Please do not…	Thoughts and Reasons	Other
Symbols				
❐ anointing oil ❐ holy water				
❐ crucifix/cross ❐ prayer shawl				
❐ fountain ❐ communion (if able)				
❐ other				
My Definition of a Good Death				
❐ family with me				
❐ friends with me				
❐ small children in room				
❐ I'm ok alone ❐ other				
❐ you're excused if you cannot stay with me				
Music				list songs/types of music
❐ I have taped music				
❐ bring specific CDs				
❐ sung by family and friends				
❐ Instrumental				
___% instrumental ___% with words				
Notify people that I would like to be there				
❐ spouse ❐ children				
❐ family ❐ friends				
❐ other				

A-1: Bedside Vigil, *continued*

Updated on_____

Circle what you desire, cross out what you do not desire, leave untouched those that are neutral.

	Please do…	Please do not…	Thoughts and Reasons	Other
Round the clock companionship ❑ yes ❑ no ❑ neutral				
Prioritize Preferred Place ___ home ___ lake cabin ___ outdoors ___ hospital ___ hospice ___ nursing home ___ other				
Talk to me about… ❑ memories ❑ heaven ❑ love ❑ who's there ❑ forgiveness ❑ what you cherish about me ❑ what you're feeling ❑ other				
Scripture I would like read ❑ Psalms ❑ Gospels ❑ about heaven ❑ other				
Other items to read to me ❑ books I have enjoyed ❑ poems ❑ other				

Notes

"Lord, remind me

how brief my time

on earth will be.

Remind me that my days are numbered,

and that my life is fleeing away.

My life is no longer than the width of my hand.

An entire lifetime is just a moment to you;

human existence is but a breath."

We are merely moving shadows,

and all our busy rushing ends in nothing.

We heap up wealth for someone else to spend.

And so, Lord, where do I put my hope?

My only hope is in you.

Psalm 39:4–7 (NLT)

Second Month

Month _____ Year _____

Sunday	Monday	Tuesday	Wednesday	Thursday	Friday	Saturday

☐ **A-2: People to notify**

☐ _____

☐ _____

☐ _____

☐ _____

☐ _____

A-2: People to Notify

Updated on _____

Look in _____ *for my most updated phone numbers.*

When to Notify	Who to Notify	How I know them	Home phone number	Cell, work, pager number	Other
Before Death or within 1–2 hours after Death ❏ Ask these people if they would like to see the body before the service (or before it is cremated).					
Within 24 hours after Death ❏ Ask these people if they would like to see the body before the service (or before it is cremated).					

A-2: People to Notify, *continued*

Updated on_____

Look in _____ *for my most updated phone numbers.*

When to Notify	Who to Notify	How I know them	Home phone number	Cell, work, pager number	Other
Before the Funeral Service					

You're all going to die,
I'm sorry to upset you,
but you're all going to die.

It's the one sure thing to look forward to.

You'll get hit by a truck while crossing the street or get salmonella from a bad piece of meat.

It's as simple as that, and we're all going to have to face the fact that we're all going to die.

Well, you're all going to die. And what are you going to leave behind when you all go to die?

When you're gone what will they find?

Just a big pile of stuff, clutched to your chest. Well, they'll auction it off and just keep the rest.

Stuff don't last, when you're gone it all goes back. It all goes back when you die.

So ask why you live life
and then try to live
like there's a why

you and I will live and will die.

Jeremiah Gamble[4]

Third Month

Month _____ Year_____

Sunday	Monday	Tuesday	Wednesday	Thursday	Friday	Saturday

☐ **A-3: About Me**

☐ _____

_____

☐ _____

☐ _____

☐ _____

☐ _____

_____

A-3: About Me

Updated on_____

Important information that only I may know

Facts:

Organ Donor ☐ Yes ☐ No **B-1: My Body**

Maiden name_____

Hometown_____

Birthplace_____

Marital status_____

Citizenship_____

Nationality_____

I am a veteran ☐ Yes ☐ No *if yes*

Service branch_____

Serial number_____

Place enlisted_____

Date enlisted_____

Wars served_____

Medals/Honors_____

Place discharged_____

Date discharged_____

VA Claim or file #_____

Other_____

_____

_____

Information for the Death Certificate

Social Security number_____

My full/legal name_____

My father's full/legal name_____

My mother's full/legal name (maiden name) _____

_____

City of Birth_____

Date of Birth_____

Highest Level of Education_____

Occupation_____

Other_____

#_____ Death Certificates needed (*total from below*)

_____ # of separate stocks   _____ # of utility bills

_____ # of bank CDs   _____ # of insurance policies

_____ # of houses   _____ # of cars

_____ # of other property   _____ # of debts

_____ # of loans

_____ # of other_____

Financial/Estate Info

Executor of will _____

Location of will _____

Insurance policies _____

_____

Location of insurance policies _____

_____

Burial insurance _____

Account information

Bank _____

Account _____

Bank _____

Account _____

Payable on Death Account at _____

Account _____

Safe Deposit Box _____

Location _____

Key is _____

Debts _____

_____

Legal issues _____

_____

_____

Location of important papers
note location of both originals and copies

Life insurance policies _____

_____

Other insurance contracts _____

_____

Stock certificates _____

_____

Savings bonds _____

_____

Other financial instruments _____

_____

_____

Birth certificate _____

_____

Marriage certificate(s) _____

_____

Divorce decree(s) _____

A-3: About Me, *continued*

Important information that only I may know

Updated on _____

Title to vehicles _____

Title to other property owned _____

Mortgage records _____

Other loan records _____

Deed to house/land _____

Business records _____

Other Bank records _____

Social Security records _____

Veteran's discharge papers _____

Earnings statements for the last year _____

Copies of the last three income tax returns filed _____

_____

Retirement plan _____

401(k) _____

IRA _____

Other papers

_____

_____

_____

_____

_____

_____

_____

_____

_____

_____

_____

_____

_____

_____

A-3: About Me, *continued*

Private info *(facts)*

Passwords

For ATM _____

For computer (home)_____

For internet_____

For computer (work)_____

For PDA/handheld computer_____

For _____   _____

For _____   _____

For _____   _____

Keys   **Location**

For vehicle_____   _____

For vehicle_____   _____

For house_____   _____

For cabin _____   _____

For work_____   _____

For _____   _____

For _____   _____

Combinations

For _____   _____

For _____   _____

For _____   _____

Hidden things

Item(s)	Where
_____	_____
_____	_____
_____	_____
_____	_____
_____	_____

Alternatively, list location of this private information

A-3: About Me, *continued*

Important information that only I may know

My immediate family

Include information about birth dates, marriage and divorce dates if desired.

Spouse_____

Children _____

Grandchildren_____

Parents_____

Brothers_____

Sisters _____

Other _____

My thoughts about heaven and death...

My Faith

Write about times that your faith was important to you, stories about encounters with God, or thoughts about faith and a "higher power".

❑ I believe in God because...

Date that I first believed in God _____

Where _____

Why _____

Date that I was baptized _____

I decided to be baptized because _____

❑ I do not believe in God because...

A-3: About Me, *continued*

Updated on_____

My thoughts about life on earth…

Books and authors that have influenced me…

Movies and plays that have influenced me…

Quotes and scripture that have spoken to me recently and throughout my life…

My Work

Write about the work you have done over your life time. What did you like to do? What did you do because you had to? And anything else that you want others to know about your work.

Retirement

Write about retirement: What has it been like for you? *OR* What do you hope it will be like?

A-3: About Me, *continued*

Important information that only I may know

Things I find funny…

My unique talents and gifts *(what I can do that is unique to me)*…

I believe that I'll be in _____ when I die.
This is what I think I'll be doing there…

What I enjoyed doing on earth…

I would like to sit down and talk with these people from history…

I want others to know these things about me…

I have enjoyed creating…

I am passionate about…

My mission statement or personal statement for life is…

I could spend hours in these stores…

I have had these struggles on earth…

Things that I find frustrating…

I lose track of time when…

Stories I enjoy telling or hearing…

A-3: About Me, *continued*

Important information that only I may know

Other _____

_____   _____
_____   _____
_____   _____
_____   _____
_____   _____
_____   _____
_____   _____
_____   _____
_____   _____
_____   _____
_____   _____
_____   _____
_____   _____
_____   _____
_____   _____
_____   _____
_____   _____
_____   _____
_____   _____
_____   _____
_____   _____
_____   _____
_____   _____

Listen,
I tell you a mystery:
We will not all sleep,
but we will all be changed—
in a flash, in the twinkling of an eye,
at the last trumpet.
For the trumpet will sound,
the dead will be raised imperishable,
and we will be changed.
...then the saying that is written
will come true:
**"Death has been
swallowed up in victory."
"Where, O death, is your victory?
Where, O death, is your sting?"**

1 Corinthians 15: 51–52, 54–55 (NIV)

Fourth Month

Month _____ Year _____

Sunday	Monday	Tuesday	Wednesday	Thursday	Friday	Saturday

☐ **A-4: Health Care Power of Attorney**

☐ Create or revise your will

☐ _____
  _____

☐ _____
  _____

☐ _____
  _____

☐ _____
  _____

A-4:
HEALTH CARE POWER OF ATTORNEY (HCPA)
Example

PRINCIPAL, _____

Birth Date: _____

Address: _____

I, _____, birth date _____, Social Security # _____, my _____, currently residing at _____, appoint _____, state of _____ (phone #_____) as my agent (my attorney in fact) to make any health care decision for me when, in the judgment of my attending physician, I am unable (physically or mentally) to make and/or communicate the decision myself and my agent consents to make and/or communicate the decision on my behalf.

If _____ predeceases me or is unwilling, unavailable, or unable to serve, then I appoint_____, my _____, currently residing at _____, state of _____, (phone #_____) as my agent.

My agent has the power to make any health care decision for me. This power includes the power to give consent, to refuse consent, or to withdraw consent to any care, treatment, service, or procedure to maintain, diagnose, or treat my physical or mental condition, including giving me food or water by artificial means. My agent has the power, where consistent with the laws of this state, to make a health care decision to withhold or stop health care necessary to keep me alive. It is my intention that my agent or any alternative agent has the personal obligation to me to make health care decisions for me consistent with my expressed wishes. I understand, however, that my agent or any alternative agent has no legal duty to act.

My agent and any alternative agents have consented to act as my agent. My agent and any alternative agents have been notified that they will be nominated as a guardian or conservator of my person.

My agent must act consistently with my desires as stated in this document or as otherwise made known by me to my agent.

My agent has the same right as I would have to receive, review, and obtain copies of my medical records and to consent to disclosure of those records.

I give my agent and alternative agents, the following additional instructions regarding my medical treatment and care:

SAMPLE ONLY   Date:_____

Signature of Principal:_____

1. I desire good pain control. If pain medication may hasten death, I still desire good pain control IF I have a terminal condition or am permanently unconscious. If pain medication may hasten death and I DO NOT have a terminal condition and am NOT permanently unconscious, I desire the best pain control available without possibility of death.

2. If I have a terminal condition OR am in a permanently unconscious state, I DO NOT want the following:

   ❑ CPR
   ❑ mechanical respiration
   ❑ kidney dialysis
   ❑ surgery (minor or major) or other invasive procedures or diagnostic tests
   ❑ transfusions of blood or blood products
   ❑ drugs or antibiotics (except pain medication)
   ❑ artificial nutrition and hydration (no feeding through IV, nasogastric, or gastrostomy, or anything similar)
   ❑ chemotherapy or other cancer treatments
   ❑ organ transplantation

3. I desire to have all possible body organs donated (to keep someone else alive, but not for research) at my death. This excludes sperm and eggs.

4. I desire to be cremated upon my death.

5. Read my charts and records. Ask questions of my providers. Be assertive.

6. I desire therapy (Occupational Therapy, Speech Therapy, Physical Therapy, Massage Therapy) as appropriate, especially if I do not have a terminal illness and am not in a permanently unconscious state.

   Make sure the therapists have my goals in mind, and that the goals are realistic and functional.

7. I am not opposed to experimental drugs or procedures as long as all options are considered and known.

8. I do not wish to have unnecessary tests or procedures done, especially if I have a terminal condition or am permanently unconscious. Do only what is necessary for accurate treatment and/or decision making; i.e. *if surgery is not an option* in light of my above wishes, then do not let them perform tests that indicate if surgery is needed.

SAMPLE ONLY

Signature of Principal:_____ Date:_____

The information contained in these documents, both individually and collectively, should not be considered legal advice. Before taking advantage of any of these documents for legal use, an individual is encouraged to consult with a knowledgeable attorney.

A-4: HEALTH CARE POWER OF ATTORNEY (HCPA)
Example, *continued*

The information contained in these documents, both individually and collectively, should not be considered legal advice. Before taking advantage of any of these documents for legal use, an individual is encouraged to consult with a knowledgeable attorney.

9. Choose the best hospital, hospice or nursing home that you think will meet my needs and the needs of family and friends. I do desire hospice care if appropriate.

10. If my judgment is impaired due to physical or mental illness and I am refusing treatments that would help me, I authorize my agent or alternative agent to force treatment on me.

11. It is impossible for me to think of every possible situation where you would be making these decisions for me; I trust your judgment and ability to discern the situation and to make decisions based on what you know about me and what you would do for yourself in the same situation. On top of all of that, I know that you will listen to God regarding what to do. He will tell you if it is my time to come to Him or not. Gather others to pray and help you.

12. **For Women:**
a. If I am known to be pregnant or found to be pregnant at any time, I DO NOT want life-sustaining treatment withheld or withdrawn if it is possible that the embryo/fetus/baby will develop to the point of live birth with the continued application of life-sustaining treatment. Therefore, if I am known or found to be pregnant I wish to be kept alive until the baby is born.

b. I DO NOT consent to an abortion at any time.

IN WITNESS WHEREOF I have signed my name this _____ day of _____, 20____.

_____   _____
TYPE YOUR NAME HERE   Signature of Principal

STATE OF _____)
)SS.
COUNTY OF _____   )

The foregoing instrument was acknowledged before me this ____ day of _____, 20 ____

By _____   _____
                                      Notary Public

OR   SAMPLE ONLY   Date:_____

Signature of Principal:_____

I certify that in my presence this _____ day of _____, 20_____, the principal, _____, signed this instrument. I am not named as agent in the instrument.

PRINTED NAME   SIGNATURE   ADDRESS

_____

_____

Original in Safe Deposit Box

At this location: _____

Address: _____

Phone #: _____

Copies located:

- ❏ car glove compartments _____
- ❏ MD _____
- ❏ Dentist _____
- ❏ day planner or PDA _____
- ❏ alternate(s) _____
- ❏ hospital record _____
- ❏ other _____

SAMPLE ONLY

Signature of Principal: _____ Date: _____

A-4:
HEALTH CARE
POWER OF
ATTORNEY (HCPA)
Example, *continued*

*The information contained
in these documents, both
individually and collectively, should not be
considered legal advice. Before taking
advantage of any of these documents for
legal use, an individual is encouraged to
consult with a knowledgeable attorney.*

My flesh and my heart may fail, but

God is the strength of my heart

and my portion forever.

Psalm 73:26 (NIV)

Fifth Month

Month:_____ Year:_____

Sunday	Monday	Tuesday	Wednesday	Thursday	Friday	Saturday

❑ **B-1: My Body**

❑ _____

❑ _____

❑ _____

❑ _____

❑ _____

B-1: My Body

Information about body decisions for my funeral

Updated on_____

Decisions to be made	Options based on decisions	Thoughts and Reasons	Other (ie. cost factors)
Living Will/Advanced Directive ❏ I have one ❏ I do not have one ❏ I am working on one	Location of the document(s)		
Health Care Power of Attorney ❏ I have one ❏ I do not have one ❏ I am working on one	Who is your HCPA?		
I want to donate my organs ❏ yes *If yes,* ❏ all or ❏ some? ❏ no ❏ undecided	If not all, specify: these are the organs that I DO want to donate		
I want to donate my body to science ❏ yes ❏ no ❏ undecided	If yes, where?		

B-1: My Body, *continued*   Updated on _____

Decisions to be made	Options based on decisions	Thoughts and Reasons	Other (ie. cost factors)
Viewing the body I want my body to be viewed at the funeral (even if it will be cremated) ❐ yes ❐ no ❐ depends	My preference for family viewing of the body ❐ viewed ❐ not viewed ❐ unsure ❐ let each individual decide	Will my loved ones grieve better if they can see the body or not?	Depends: this decision may depend on a variety of situations. Who can get to the funeral and when. What does your family want? Check "depends" if you have a preference, but under certain circumstances would prefer that other options be used.
Burial I want to be buried at Cemetery location_____ (military plot, local plot, hometown plot) Phone _____ Funeral Home Contact Phone _____ Name _____	I want the following to decorate my casket ❐ pall ❐ flowers ❐ other I want the body present at ❐ the wake only ❐ the wake and funeral ❐ not present for public viewing		
I want the following type of casket ❐ simple, inexpensive ❐ wood ❐ metal ❐ rental (for cremation) ❐ other_____	❐ least expensive ❐ moderate expense ❐ cost does not matter		

Decisions to be made	Options based on decisions	Thoughts and Reasons	Other (ie. cost factors)
Cremation I want the body to be cremated ❐ yes ❐ no ❐ undecided Crematory contact Name_____ Phone_____ Funeral home contact Name_____ Phone_____ I want my family present at cremation ❐ yes ❐ no ❐ other_____ I want ashes present at memorial service ❐ yes ❐ no ❐ other_____	I want the body present at ❐ the wake only ❐ the wake and funeral ❐ not present for public viewing I want cremation to occur ❐ as soon after death as possible ❐ after a family viewing ❐ after a public viewing ❐ after the funeral ❐ other_____ I want the ashes placed ❐ urn in home ❐ urn placed at cemetery _____ *Location* _____ *Phone* ❐ scattered at _____ ❐ other _____		If your body is cremated, there are still many options for your family and friends to view your body. And even if there is not a viewing, you may decide to have the body dressed for cremation. Consider each of the "Decisions to be made" sections for these reasons. An urn can be placed at a cemetery, either in a niche in a mausoleum or buried outside.
I want my body to be embalmed ❐ yes ❐ no ❐ other_____	Under which conditions? ❐ all ❐ other_____		A public viewing may mean that your body must be embalmed.

B-1: My Body, *continued*   Updated on_____

Decisions to be made	Options based on decisions	Thoughts and Reasons	Other (ie. cost factors)
I want the committal service to be the same day as the funeral: ❐ yes ❐ no ❐ other_____	I want this service to be open to the following ❐ family only ❐ open to all ❐ other		May depend on the season of the year. Would you rather have your committal service in the Spring or as soon as possible after the service?
I want my eye glasses to be ❐ on ❐ off ❐ NA	For ❐ reviewal ❐ burial ❐ cremation		
I want my body to be dressed in (specify the clothing you desire)	I want the clothing removed before burial or cremation ❐ yes ❐ no		
I want a DNA sample taken from my body ❐ yes ❐ no	Under which conditions? ❐ all ❐ other		
I desire an autopsy be performed ❐ yes ❐ no	Under which conditions? ❐ all ❐ other ❐ accident ❐ sudden death		
Other			

"I have told you all this
so that you may have peace in me.
Here on earth
you will have many trials
and sorrows.

But take heart, because

I have overcome
the world."

–Jesus

John 16:33 (NLT)

Sixth Month

Month:_____   Year:_____

Sunday	Monday	Tuesday	Wednesday	Thursday	Friday	Saturday

☐ **B-2: Funeral To Do list**

☐ **B-3: Care Calendar**

☐ _____

☐ _____

☐ _____

☐ _____

B-2: Funeral To Do List

Updated on _____

Before Death or Within One or Two Hours After Death

☐ Call designated person(s) to help with this list.

Name _____

Phone _____

Alternate _____

Phone _____

☐ Call my church

Contact name _____

Phone _____

☐ Call first group of people on the contact list (before death or within 1–2 hours after death), **A-2: People to Notify**.

☐ Give a copy of the Care Calendar for my family member to these accountability people, **B-3: Care Calendar**.

1. Name _____

Phone _____

2. Name _____

Phone _____

3. Name _____

Phone _____

☐ Call the funeral home _____

Contact name _____

Phone _____

☐ Ask hospital or funeral home staff to make arrangements for organ donation, **B-1: My Body**.

☐ Ask funeral home staff to make arrangements to donate the body to science, **B-1: My Body**. I desire the body donated to

_____

☐ Arrange for an autopsy to be performed, **B-1: My Body**.

☐ Give list of **B-1: My Body** details to the funeral home director and a pastor.

☐ Find the most recent forms and ideas for my funeral in

_____

☐ Find important papers and numbers in

_____

_____

☐ Order _____ # of Death Certificates, **A-3: About Me**.

☐ Other _____

_____

☐ Other _____

_____

Within Twenty-Four Hours After Death

❐ Finalize the place and times of the wake and funeral,
See my planning form for help, **B-6: The Funeral Service**.

❐ Place the obituary in the following newspapers, **C-5: Obituary, Eulogy and Grave Marker**.

Primary newspaper _____

Phone _____

Other newspapers _____

Phone _____

Phone _____

  ❐ Use my words on the obituary form

  ❐ Use a traditional format

❐ Finalize the pastor(s) to lead the service, **B-6: The Funeral Service**

My preferences _____

❐ Give the following planning forms to the pastor who will be leading the service:

      ❐ **A-3: About Me**
      ❐ **B-6: The Funeral Service**
      ❐ **B-7: The Committal Service**
      ❐ **C-1: Songs and Music**
      ❐ **C-2: Scripture and Readings**
      ❐ **C-3: Prayer**
      ❐ **C-4: Symbols and Mementos**
      ❐ **C-5: Obituary, Eulogy and Grave Marker**
      ❐ **C-6: Order of Service**
      ❐ **C-7: My Funeral Program**

❐ Call the people to be notified within 24 hours after death, **A-2: People to Notify**.

❐ Arrange for someone to stay at my house for security purposes.

❐ Arrange for child care for the decision maker's children if needed. Do not bring children while making decisions with the pastor or funeral home staff.

❐ Money to pay for the funeral can be found in **A-3: About Me**

  ❐ Prepayment at funeral home. The agreement/contract is located

_____

  ❐ Prepayment of property at cemetery. Agreement/contract located

_____

  ❐ A bank account that is payable on death is at:

_____

  ❐ A Life Insurance policy _____

    naming _____

    as beneficiary.

  ❐ Other _____

_____

  ❐ Other _____

_____

Updated on_____

The Day after Death

❐ Find musicians, **B-6: The Funeral Service**.

My suggestions _____

❐ Give the musicians the list of songs and music and tapes or CDs made, **C-1: Songs and Music**. Tapes and CDs for my funeral are located

_____

❐ Arrange for the meal of consolation, **C-8: The Meal of Consolation**

❐ Order flowers from _____

Spend no more than $_____

B-5: Cost Planning Form, **B-7: The Committal Service**, **C-4: Symbols and Mementos**, **C-6: Order of Service** contain details on types of flowers.

❐ Arrange for _____ for each person attending. for **Candles/Roses to Cross** portion of service, **Introduction**, **C-6: Order of Service**, **C-7: My Funeral Program**.

Estimated number of items needed _____

❐ Decide on people to read at the service, **B-6: The Funeral Service**, **B7: The Committal Service**

Names of potential readers

_____

_____

_____

❐ Give a copy of **C-2: Scripture and Readings** planning form to those who will read.

❐ Have one person coordinate the readings with the pastor, **B-6: The Funeral Service**.

Name _____

❐ Make final changes to the program with the pastor, **C-7: My Funeral Program**.

❐ Call an attorney and/or trust officer if needed.

❐ I have an attorney

Name _____

Phone_____

❐ I have a trust officer

Name _____

Phone_____

❐ I do not have a designated attorney or trust officer.

❐ Other _____

_____

❐ Other _____

_____

Second Day after Death

❐ Check the funeral binder for any letters, videos or tapes that I have made that need to be distributed to others before the funeral service. Distribute these no less than one or two days before the service, **B-4: Goodbye Letters/Tapes/Videos**.

❐ Have the program printed or copied and folded. Make _____ copies.

The original is located _____

C-7: My Funeral Program, B-5: Cost Planning Form.

❐ Have the folders made (from the funeral home). Make _____ copies.

The original is located _____

B-5: Cost Planning Form.

❐ Have the acknowledgement cards made. Make _____ copies.

The original is located _____

B-5: Cost Planning Form,
C-5: Obituary, Eulogy and Grave Marker.

❐ Decide if taped music will be played at the wake, funeral and/or committal service, **C-1: Songs and Music**.

❐ Gather the symbols and mementos that I have specified on the planning form, **C-4: Symbols and Mementos**.

❐ Call the rest of the people on the list: **A-2: People to Notify**.

❐ Plan the committal service. Decide if the committal service will be the same day of the funeral service or on a different day, **B-7: The Committal Service, B-1: My Body**.

❐ If the committal service is on a different day than the funeral, make plans to have people available to support my family.

❐ Other _____

_____

❐ Other _____

_____

❐ Other _____

_____

Within The First Thirty Days After Death

❏ Notify all of my doctors and health care providers of my death.

Primary Doctor _____

  Phone_____

Specialist _____

  Phone_____

Dentist_____

  Phone_____

Other _____

  Phone_____

❏ Notify my life insurance agent.

Name _____

Phone_____

❏ File claim for life insurance benefits.

❏ Call Social Security at 1-800-772-1213 to report my death.

Do not cash the Social Security checks in my name from the month that death occurred or after.

For my spouse: if you were receiving Social Security checks, call the Social Security office before you cash your first check after my death and confirm that the amount is correct.

❏ If I was employed at time of death, contact the Human Resource Department to check on wages and payment for unused vacation that may be available.

❏ Call an attorney, if needed, to settle the estate.

❏ File for other benefits:

  ❏ Veteran's benefits

  ❏ Retirement plan benefits

  ❏ Employer-sponsored life insurance benefits

  ❏ Other life insurance benefits

  ❏ Credit insurance benefits

  ❏ Automobile insurance benefits

  ❏ Social and/or fraternal organization benefits

❏ Check on any insurance premium refunds my spouse or family may be entitled to receive.

❏ Change the name on property titles. This may feel disloyal; however it is very important for financial reasons.

❏ Access my safe deposit box.

❏ Cancel all credit cards in my name.

❏ Purchase a grave marker.

❏ Remove my name from all joint banking accounts. Transfer these accounts to those living only.

❏ Other _____

_____

Within The First Twelve Months After Death

❏ Decide if you (my spouse, family or roommate) will stay in current house or move.

❏ Give my clothes to _____

_____

_____

❏ Consider getting a pet.

❏ Join a grief support group three to four months after my death.

❏ Hire a housekeeper and someone to help with yard work.

❏ Other _____

_____

_____

❏ Other _____

_____

_____

❏ Other _____

_____

_____

B-3: Care Calendar 1

Updated on _____

For _____   *Accountability Person* _____
　　　　　　　　(name)

Here is a plan for you to take care of yourself after I am gone.

Remember _____

_____

_____

Each Day

1. _____

2. _____

3. _____

4. _____

5. _____

6. _____

Day 1	Day 2	Day 3
Day 8	Day 9	Day 10
Day 15	Day 16	Day 17
Day 22	Day 23	Day 24
Day 29	Day 30	Day 31

B-3: Care Calendar 1, *continued*   Updated on _____

Other thoughts for you _____

_____

Day 4	Day 5	Day 6	Day 7
Day 11	Day 12	Day 13	Day 14
Day 18	Day 19	Day 20	Day 21
Day 25	Day 26	Day 27	Day 28
Day 32	Day 33	Day 34	Day 35

B-3: Care Calendar 2

Updated on _____

For _____
(name)

Accountability Person _____

Here is a plan for you to take care of yourself after I am gone.

Remember _____

_____

_____

Each Day

1. _____

2. _____

3. _____

4. _____

5. _____

6. _____

Day 1	Day 2	Day 3
Day 8	Day 9	Day 10
Day 15	Day 16	Day 17
Day 22	Day 23	Day 24
Day 29	Day 30	Day 31

B-3: Care Calendar 2, *continued*

Other thoughts for you _____
_____

Day 4	Day 5	Day 6	Day 7
Day 11	Day 12	Day 13	Day 14
Day 18	Day 19	Day 20	Day 21
Day 25	Day 26	Day 27	Day 28
Day 32	Day 33	Day 34	Day 35

B-3: Care Calendar 3

Updated on _____

For _____
(name)

Accountability Person _____

Here is a plan for you to take care of yourself after I am gone.

Remember _____

_____

_____

Each Day

1. _____

2. _____

3. _____

4. _____

5. _____

6. _____

Day 1	Day 2	Day 3
Day 8	Day 9	Day 10
Day 15	Day 16	Day 17
Day 22	Day 23	Day 24
Day 29	Day 30	Day 31

B-3: Care Calendar 3, *continued*

Updated on _____

Other thoughts for you _____

_____

Day 4	Day 5	Day 6	Day 7
Day 11	Day 12	Day 13	Day 14
Day 18	Day 19	Day 20	Day 21
Day 25	Day 26	Day 27	Day 28
Day 32	Day 33	Day 34	Day 35

Come to Me I am the comforter
Come crawl up upon My knee
Lay your head close against My heart
Find your rest in Me.

When it hurts too much to cry I will hold you
When you feel that you will never make it through
When you need someone to turn to
I'll enfold you in my arms
For my child I love you
Chorus

When the days are long
and the nights feel so empty
In the loneliness I'll stay by your side
When you can't explain your feelings
I'll listen to your heart
I will hear the thoughts you hide
Chorus

When the time is right you will know My healing
For I am the hope that never dies
I am Christ the Lord who lives forever
And in Me even the dead will arise
Chorus

Maureen Pranghofer and Dan Adler[5]

Seventh Month

Month:_____   Year:_____

Sunday	Monday	Tuesday	Wednesday	Thursday	Friday	Saturday

❏ **B-4: Goodbye Letters/Tapes/ Videos**

❏ **B-5: Cost Planning Form**

❏ _____

❏ _____

❏ _____

❏ _____

B-4: **Goodbye Letters/Tapes/Videos**   Updated on _____

For (LIST NAMES)	Target Date for Completion	Letter/Audio Video/Other	Location	Give to	Other
Spouse		❏ letter ❏ audio tape ❏ video tape ❏ other_____		❏ before funeral ❏ at graveside ❏ other_____	
Children		❏ letter ❏ audio tape ❏ video tape ❏ other_____		❏ before funeral ❏ at graveside ❏ at graduation ❏ at wedding ❏ other_____	
Family		❏ letter ❏ audio tape ❏ video tape ❏ other_____		❏ before funeral ❏ at graveside ❏ other_____	
Friends		❏ Letter ❏ Audio Tape ❏ Video Tape ❏ Other_____		❏ before funeral ❏ at graveside ❏ other_____	
People with whom you struggled		❏ letter ❏ audio tape ❏ video tape ❏ other_____		❏ before funeral ❏ at graveside ❏ other_____	
Other		❏ letter ❏ audio tape ❏ video tape ❏ other_____		❏ before funeral ❏ at graveside ❏ other_____	

B-5: Cost Planning Form

Updated on_____

Item	Cost Expectations	Prepaid at Funeral Home	Cost Limits I desire	Thoughts and Reasons	Actual Costs	Other
TOTAL amount for the funeral						
Services of funeral director and staff						
Cremation of the body						
Burial of the body						
Body preparation Embalming Hairstylist						
Casket ❑ buy or ❑ rent						❑Already purchased. Located
Casket bearers						
Visitation, for family only						
Visitation, for the public						
Transportation of remains						

B-5: Cost Planning Form, *continued*

Updated on _____

Item	Cost Expectations	Prepaid at Funeral Home	Cost Limits I desire	Thoughts and Reasons	Actual Costs	Other
Funeral hearse						
Procession lead car						
Family car						
Service support vehicle						
Limousine						
Classic car						
Other transportation						
Urn						❏ Already purchased. Located
Burial vault						
Cemetery plot or place for ashes						
Headstone or marker						
Rental of room for wake						

B-5: Cost Planning Form, *continued*   Updated on_____

Item	Cost Expectations	Prepaid at Funeral Home	Cost Limits I desire	Thoughts and Reasons	Actual Costs	Other
Rental of room for funeral						
Honorarium for pastor(s)						
Honorarium for musician(s)						
Register book (guest book)						❑ Already purchased. Located
Folders						
Printing/folding of program/ bulletin						
Acknowledgement cards						
Flowers						
Other decorations						
Other funeral home expenses						
Obituary (total for all papers)						

B-5: Cost Planning Form, *continued*   Updated on_____

Item	Cost Expectations	Prepaid at Funeral Home	Cost Limits I desire	Thoughts and Reasons	Actual Costs	Other
Food for the meal of consolation (amount per person times number of people expected)						
Purchase of music (if needed)						
Audio tape recording of service						
Video tape recording of service						
Internet service						
Memorial merchandise						
Forwarding of remains						
Receiving of remains						
Immediate burial						

B-5: Cost Planning Form, *continued*   Updated on _____

Item	Cost Expectations	Prepaid at Funeral Home	Cost Limits I desire	Thoughts and Reasons	Actual Costs	Other
Direct cremation						
Certified copies of death certificate						
Cemetery grave opening fee						
Marker setting fee						
Crematory charges						
Air transportation charges						
Other transportation (from out-of-state)						
Procession escort						
Other						
Other						

"For I know the plans
    I have for you," says the Lord.
They are plans for good
    and not for disaster,
        to give you **a future and a hope**.
            In those days when you pray,
                I will listen.
                If you look for me in earnest,
                    you will find me
                        when you seek me.
                    I will be found by you,"
                        says the Lord.
                I will end your captivity
            and restore your fortunes.
    I will gather you out of the nations
where I sent you
and bring you home again
    to your own land."

Jeremiah 29:11–14 (NLT)

Eighth Month

Month:_____   Year:_____

Sunday	Monday	Tuesday	Wednesday	Thursday	Friday	Saturday

☐ **B-6: The Funeral Service**

☐ **B-7: The Committal Service**

☐ _____

☐ _____

☐ _____

☐ _____

B-6: The Funeral Service

Updated on_____

Detail	Cost Limits that I Desire	Specifics	Thoughts and Reasons	Other Items to Consider
Theme		❑ Veteran: ❑ Military ❑ Non-Military ❑ Christian ❑ Non-Christian ❑ Jewish ❑ Other_____ ❑ Traditional_____ ❑ Non-traditional_____ Prioritize (1, 2, 3, etc.) emphasis on: ____ comfort ____ celebration ____ forgiveness ____ reconciliation ____ worship ____ sharing ____ teaching and evangelism ____ joy ____ eulogizing ____ other_____		
Atmosphere		Prioritize (1, 2, 3, etc.) emphasis on ____ comfortable ____ familiar ____ beautiful ____ traditional ____ easy location ____ welcoming ____ safe ____ truthful ____ other_____		

Detail	Cost Limits that I Desire	Specifics	Thoughts and Reasons	Other Items to Consider
Place for service		Prioritize (1, 2, 3, etc.) locations of the service: ____ funeral home _____ ____ church _____ ____ cemetery _____ ____ home _____ ____ restaurant _____ ____ golf course _____ ____ other _____ ____ a familiar place ____ a practical place ____ a comforting place		Religious symbols present Facilities available for food
Place for wake		Same or different location than the service? Prioritize (1, 2, 3, etc.) locations of the wake ____ funeral home _____ ____ church _____ ____ cemetery _____ ____ home _____ ____ restaurant _____ ____ golf course _____ ____ other _____ ____ a familiar place ____ a practical place ____ a comforting place		Religious symbols present Place to eat Cost can affect decision about time and place

Detail	Cost Limits that I Desire	Specifics	Thoughts and Reasons	Other Items to Consider
Timing		Wake ❏ evening before the funeral service ❏ one or two hours before the funeral service ❏ both of the above ❏ other_____ Funeral ❏ as soon as possible after death ❏ 3–5 days after death ❏ 1–2 weeks after death ❏ 1 month after death ❏ weekday ❏ weekend ❏ other_____ Time of day ❏ AM ❏ PM Specifics_____ *NOT* on these dates or events: _____		Cost can impact timing Indicate if you do not want the service on a certain holiday or event day (birthday, etc.)
People to lead the service		Pastor or lay staff 1._____ 2._____ 3._____		
People to host the wake		1._____ 2._____		

Detail	Cost Limits that I Desire	Specifics	Thoughts and Reasons	Other Items to Consider
People to lead prayer		1._____ 2._____ 3._____		
People to plan and read scripture		1._____ 2._____ 3._____		The person planning the readings does not need to be the same person that reads. Indicate if you will have a separate planner for this task.
Pallbearers		1._____ 2._____ 3._____ 4._____ 5._____ 6._____		Actual or honorary or both

B-6: The Funeral Service, *continued*

Updated on_____

Detail	Cost Limits that I Desire	Specifics	Thoughts and Reasons	Other Items to Consider
Musicians		1._____ 2._____ 3._____		
Person to plan music		1._____ 2._____		
Worship leader		1._____ 2._____		
Singers		1._____ 2._____		
Soloist		1._____ 2._____		
Instrumentalists		1._____ 2._____		

Detail	Cost Limits that I Desire	Specifics	Thoughts and Reasons	Other Items to Consider
Allocation of memorial funds		____% to defray expenses ____% to go to _____ ____% to _____ ____% to _____ ____% to _____ ❑ give anonymously ❑ okay to be recognized ❑ other_____		
Rituals and/or Traditions		Wake ❑ poster of photos ❑ casket open ❑ coffee and tea served ❑ chairs available for guests ❑ other_____ Funeral ❑ casket at the front of the church ❑ family escorted in by pastor or funeral home director or_____ ❑ casket closed ❑ casket open ❑ other_____		

B-6: The Funeral Service, *continued*   Updated on_____

Detail	Cost Limits that I Desire	Specifics	Thoughts and Reasons	Other Items to Consider
Other				
Other				
Other				

B-7: The Committal Service

Updated on_____

Detail	Cost Limits that I Desire	Specifics	Thoughts and Reasons	Other Items to Consider
Theme		❑ Veteran: ❑ Military ❑ Non-Military ❑ Christian ❑ Non-Christian ❑ Jewish ❑ other _____ ❑ traditional_____ ❑ non-traditional_____		
Atmosphere		Prioritize (1, 2, 3, etc.) emphasis on ____ solemn ____ informal ____ traditional ____ other_____		
Place for committal service		Prioritize (1, 2, 3, etc.) desired place ____ cemetery _____ lot_____ contact _____ phone _____ ____ other location _____		Religious symbols present Season Where to scatter or bury the ashes if the body is cremated

Detail	Cost Limits that I Desire	Specifics	Thoughts and Reasons	Other Items to Consider
Timing		Day ❏ same day of funeral ❏ day after funeral ❏ wait for a certain season or time 　　❏ summer　❏ spring 　　❏ winter　❏ fall　OR 　　❏_____ Time of day ❏ AM ❏ PM Specifics_____ NOT on these dates or events _____		Cost can impact timing Indicate if you do not want the service on a certain holiday or event day (birthday, etc.)
People to lead the service		Pastor or lay staff 1._____ 2._____ 3._____		
Music		❏ instrumental ❏ praise ❏ worship ❏ other_____		Live or recorded? For those present (to listen) or for participation by those present?

B-7: The Committal Service, *continued*   Updated on_____

Detail	Cost Limits that I Desire	Specifics	Thoughts and Reasons	Other Items to Consider
Readings: Scripture, Prayer and other readings		❏ scripture ❏ prayer ❏ other		
People to read scripture, prayers or other readings		1._____ 2._____ 3._____		
Pallbearers		1._____ 2._____ 3._____ 4._____ 5._____ 6._____		Actual or honorary or both
Symbols/ decorations		❏ flowers ❏ pall ❏ crucifix or cross ❏ balloons ❏ other		

Detail	Cost Limits that I Desire	Specifics	Thoughts and Reasons	Other Items to Consider
Hearse (if applicable)		Type ❑ traditional ❑ classic car ❑ other_____		
Transportation for family		Type ❑ limousine ❑ traditional vehicle from funeral home ❑ classic car ❑ our family car ❑ other _____		

Rituals and/ or traditions		❑ Seated service
		❑ Everyone there puts a shovel full of dirt on casket/urn
		❑ Roses or other flowers placed on casket/urn
		   ❑ before burial
		   ❑ after buried
		❑ All leave before casket/urn is placed
		❑ All stay until casket/urn is placed
		❑ All scatter some of the ashes
		❑ Some ashes scattered and some kept
		❑ Other_____		

Other				

And I heard a voice
from heaven saying,
"Write this down:
**Blessed are those
who die in the Lord**
from now on.

Yes, says the Spirit,
they are blessed indeed,
for they will rest
from all their toils and trials;
for their good deeds
follow them!"

Revelation 14:13 (NLT)

Soon and very soon, we are going to see the King.

Soon and very soon, we are going to see the King.

Soon and very soon, we are going to see the King.

Hallelujah, Hallelujah, we are going to see the King.

No more crying there, we are going to see the King.

No more crying there, we are going to see the King.

No more crying there, we are going to see the King.

Hallelujah, Hallelujah, we are going to see the King.

No more dying there, we are going to see the King.

No more dying there, we are going to see the King.

No more dying there, we are going to see the King.

Hallelujah, Hallelujah, we are going to see the King.

**Hallelujah, Hallelujah,
we are going
to see the King.**

Andrae Crouch[6]

Ninth Month

Month:_____ Year:_____

Sunday	Monday	Tuesday	Wednesday	Thursday	Friday	Saturday

☐ **C-1: Songs and Music**

☐ **C-2: Scripture and Readings**

☐ _____

☐ _____

☐ _____

☐ _____

C-1: Songs and Music

Updated on_____

Song/Music Type	Title	Why I like it or want it in my funeral
Comforting		
Early years of faith or life		
Favorites		
Instrumentals		

C-1: Songs and Music, *continued*

Updated on_____

List the version preferred. List the CD or tape that it's on.	For the service	For the bedside vigil	For the wake	For the graveside	Other times	Words and music taped or in my binder?

C-1: Songs and Music, *continued*   Updated on_____

Song/Music Type	Title	Why I like it or want it in my funeral
Forgiveness or love		
Life		
Heaven, God or the afterlife		
Death		

C-1: Songs and Music, *continued*

Updated on_____

List the version preferred. List the CD or tape that it's on.	For the service	For the bedside vigil	For the wake	For the graveside	Other times	Words and music taped or in my binder?

C-1: Songs and Music, *continued*

Updated on_____

Song/Music Type		Title	Why I like it or want it in my funeral
Prayer and meditation			
Other			
Other			
Other			

C-1: Songs and Music, *continued*

Updated on_____

List the version preferred. List the CD or tape that it's on.	For the service	For the bedside vigil	For the wake	For the graveside	Other times	Words and music taped or in my binder?

C-2: Scripture and Readings

Updated on _____

Scripture or Reading	Reference and key words	Why I like it or want it in my funeral	Use this version of the Bible	For the service	For the bedside vigil	For the wake	For the graveside	Other times
Comforting								
Early years of faith or life								
Favorites								
Death								

C-2: Scripture and Readings, *continued*   Updated on_____

Scripture or Reading	Reference and key words	Why I like it or want it in my funeral	Use this version of the Bible	For the service	For the bedside vigil	For the wake	For the graveside	Other times
Prayer and Meditation								
Forgiveness and love								
Life								
Heaven, God or the afterlife								

C-2: Scripture and Readings, *continued*   Updated on_____

Scripture or Reading	Reference and key words	Why I like it or want it in my funeral	Use this version of the Bible	For the service	For the bedside vigil	For the wake	For the graveside	Other times
Favorite Psalms or poems								
Praise and worship								
Quotes from other sources								
Thanks								

C-2: **Scripture and Readings**, *continued*   Updated on_____

Scripture or Reading	Reference and key words	Why I like it or want it in my funeral	Use this version of the Bible	For the service	For the bedside vigil	For the wake	For the graveside	Other times
Hopes for my family and the world								
Other								
Other								
Other								

The Lord is my shepherd; I have everything I need.

He lets me rest in green meadows;
he leads me beside peaceful streams.
He renews my strength.
He guides me along right paths,
bringing honor to his name.
Even when I walk through
the dark valley of death,
I will not be afraid,
for you are close beside me.
Your rod and your staff
protect and comfort me.
You prepare a feast for me
in the presence of my enemies.
You welcome me as a guest,
anointing my head with oil.
My cup overflows with blessings.
Surely your goodness
and unfailing love will pursue me
all the days of my life,
and I will live in the house
of the Lord forever.

Psalm 23 (NLT)

God, my shepherd! I don't need a thing.
You have bedded me down in lush
meadows, you find me quiet pools
to drink from.
True to your word,
you let me catch my breath and
send me in the right direction.
Even when the way goes
through Death Valley,
I'm not afraid
when you walk at my side.
Your trusty shepherd's crook
makes me feel secure.
You serve me a six-course dinner
right in front of my enemies.
You revive my drooping head;
my cup brims with blessing.
Your beauty and love chase
after me every day of my life.
I'm back home in the house of God
for the rest of my life.

Psalm 23 (MSG)

Tenth Month

Month:_____   Year:_____

Sunday	Monday	Tuesday	Wednesday	Thursday	Friday	Saturday

☐ **C-3: Prayer**

☐ **C-4: Symbols and Mementos**

☐ _____

☐ _____

☐ _____

☐ _____

C-3: Prayer

Updated on_____

Prayer Type	Key Words	Reference location of prayer (NA if spontaneous)	For the service	For the bedside vigil	For the wake	For the graveside	Other times
For comfort							
About death							
In Praise of God or life							

C-3: Prayer, *continued*

Updated on_____

Prayer Type	Key Words	Reference location of prayer (NA if spontaneous)	For the service	For the bedside vigil	For the wake	For the graveside	Other times
About forgiveness or love							
About God's sovereignty							
Favorites							

C-3: Prayer, *continued*

Updated on_____

Prayer Type	Key Words	Reference location of prayer (NA if spontaneous)	For the service	For the bedside vigil	For the wake	For the graveside	Other times
For your loved ones							
Other							
Other							

I am coming soon....

I will write on him
the name of my God
and the name of
the city of my God,
the new Jerusalem,
which is coming down
out of heaven
from my God;
and I will also write
on him my new name.

Revelation 3:11–12 (NIV)

C-4: Symbols and Mementos

Updated on_____

Object	Why important to me	Location	For the service	For the bedside vigil	For the wake	For the committal service	Other
Religious symbols ❑ cross ❑ crucifix ❑ pall ❑ prayer shawl ❑ icons ❑ candles ❑ other_____							
Flowers ❑ roses ❑ daisies ❑ wildflowers ❑ tulips ❑ whatever is in season ❑ other_____							
Pictures/paintings							
Photos ❑ wedding ❑ graduation ❑ vacation ❑ family ❑ other_____							

C-4: Symbols and Mementos, *continued*   Updated on_____

Object	Why important to me	Location	For the service	For the bedside vigil	For the wake	For the committal service	Other
Objects representing comfort ❑ blankets ❑ my favorite chair ❑ stuffed animal/toy ❑ pillows ❑ other							
Objects of celebration ❑ balloons ❑ bells/chimes ❑ cake ❑ champagne ❑ other							
Objects that represent heaven or eternity to me ❑ fork in hand ❑ picture of heaven ❑ other							
Objects for prayer and meditation ❑ fountain ❑ cross ❑ crucifix ❑ candles ❑ incense ❑ other							

C-4: Symbols and Mementos, *continued*   Updated on_____

Object	Why important to me	Location	For the service	For the bedside vigil	For the wake	For the committal service	Other
Gifts from others that have been meaningful to me							
Other							
Other							
Other							

Jesus said to her,

"I am the resurrection and the life;

he who believes

in Me will live

even if he dies,

and everyone who lives

and believes in Me

will never die.

Do you believe this?"

John 11:25–26 (NASB)

Eleventh Month

Month:_____ Year:_____

Sunday	Monday	Tuesday	Wednesday	Thursday	Friday	Saturday

☐ **C-5: Obituary, Eulogy and Grave Marker**

☐ **C-6: Order of Service**

☐ _____

☐ _____

☐ _____

☐ _____

C-5: Obituary, Eulogy and Grave Marker   Updated on _____

Obituary:

Specifics: write detailed information as needed.
If more room is needed, use the next page to fill in details.

Who I want to make the final determination on
what is written

☐ Spouse   ☐ Parent   ☐ Child   ☐ Friend

☐ Pastor   ☐ Other _____
                                    name

Traditional

In which newspaper(s) _____

_____

Cost: ☐ spend minimally   ☐ maximum of $_____

Photo: Recent or from _____

Name/nickname(s) _____

_____

Maiden name (nee)_____
Date of   Birth
birth _____   place _____
Date of
death_____   Age _____
Resident
of (city)_____

Died of/cause of death _____

Occupation_____

Church membership _____

Other memberships _____

Military service _____
_____

Preceded in death by _____
_____
_____
_____
_____
_____
_____

Survived by (name, relationship, city, state) _____
_____
_____
_____
_____
_____
_____

Do not include _____
_____
_____
_____

Other_____
_____
_____
_____

C-5: Obituary, Eulogy and Grave Marker, *continued*

Updated on_____

My Own Obituary Version

Circle the items from the version on the preceding page that you want in your obituary. Use these items along with the following.
Write out what you would like said about you, including any special quotes from books or verses from scripture.
Note if you wish them written out or just referenced.

_____
_____
_____
_____
_____
_____
_____
_____
_____
_____
_____
_____
_____
_____
_____
_____
_____
_____
_____
_____
_____
_____
_____
_____
_____

C-5: Obituary, Eulogy and Grave Marker, *continued*

Updated on_____

Eulogy

Specifics: write detailed information as needed. If more room is needed, use the next page to fill in details.

Who I want to make the final determination on what is said

☐ Spouse   ☐ Parent   ☐ Child   ☐ Friend

☐ Pastor   ☐ Other_____

                                       name

I want #_____ eulogies.

I want these people to speak at (fill in: funeral, vigil, meal, committal or other).

1. _____at_____

2. _____at_____

3. _____at_____

4. _____at_____

5. _____at_____

Start with a favorite quote or scripture

_____

_____

_____

_____

_____

_____died on _____

      My name   *this date*

of _____ from_____

   this year

_____

_____

My life on earth and what I expect in heaven or after death

_____

_____

Some facts_____

_____

_____

My heritage is_____

_____

_____

I was trained as_____

_____

_____

I want to say this about my marriage(s)_____

_____

_____

I want to say this about my children_____

_____

C-5: Obituary, Eulogy and Grave Marker, *continued*

Updated on_____

Other facts I want mentioned _____
_____
_____

My spouse _____
_____
_____

Quotes that describe my life on earth and/or my faith _____
_____
_____

My goal(s) in life _____
_____
_____

I struggled with _____
_____
_____

These things delighted me _____
_____
_____

I want to say these things about my faith _____
_____
_____

I want to say these things to the people at my funeral _____
_____
_____

My Own Eulogy Version

Circle the items from the version on the preceding page that you want in your eulogy. Use these items along with the following. Write out what you would like said about you, including any special quotes from books or verses from scripture. Note if you wish them written out or just referenced.

_____
_____
_____
_____
_____
_____
_____
_____
_____
_____
_____
_____
_____
_____
_____
_____
_____
_____
_____
_____
_____
_____

C-5: Obituary, Eulogy and Grave Marker, *continued*

Updated on_____

Grave Marker

Who I want to make the final determination on
what is written

❑ Spouse ❑ Parent ❑ Child ❑ Friend
❑ Pastor ❑ Other_____

My name _____

Birth date_____

Date of death_____

Other _____

Scripture _____

Words_____

Type of Marker

❑ large ❑ medium ❑ small

❑ above ground ❑ ground level

❑ stone _____

❑ color_____

❑ other_____

Thank you cards, acknowledgement cards

Who I want to make the final determination on
what is written

❑ Spouse ❑ Parent ❑ Child ❑ Friend
❑ Pastor ❑ Other_____

Ideas _____
_____

Symbols_____
_____

Words_____
_____

Quotations _____
_____

Other_____
_____
_____

C-6: Order of Service

Updated on_____

Item (cross out the items that will not apply to your service)	Suggested	Order I desire	Thoughts and Specific Details	Other
Arranging symbols	prior			
Guest book	prior			
Hand out programs	prior			
Hand out votive candles, roses or _____	prior			
Prelude	first			
Welcome	second			
Prayer	third			
Meditative prayer or music	fourth			
Scripture Readings	middle			
Worship	middle			
Eulogy and meditation	middle			

C-6: Order of Service, *continued*

Updated on_____

Item (cross out the items that will not apply to your service)	Suggested	Order I desire	Thoughts and Specific Details	Other
Time for Sharing (open mike or scripted)	after eulogy			Options to "open mike" are sharing via video tape at the meal, cards passed during the service for remembrances, and sharing at the graveside.
Instrumentals	during candles/ roses to cross			
Worship	middle			
Scripture readings	middle			
Prayer for those left	near end			
Instrumentals	during prayer for those left			
Worship	near end			
Postlude	end			
Meal of consolation	after service or immediately following the committal service			
Committal service	before or after meal OR on a different day		Consider timing: if the committal service is on the same day as the funeral, there may need to be a "rush" to get to the cemetery on time before or after the meal.	
Other				

Love generously,

praise loudly,

live fully.

Elias Porter[7]

Twelfth Month

Month:_____ Year:_____

Sunday	Monday	Tuesday	Wednesday	Thursday	Friday	Saturday

☐ **C-7: My Funeral Program**

☐ **C-8: The Meal of Consolation**

☐ _____

_____

☐ _____

_____

☐ _____

_____

☐ _____

_____

C-7: My Funeral Program

Updated on_____

Page	Graphics or Photos	Words *Note Preferred Font*	Color or B/W	Thoughts and Reasons	Other
The cover			❑ Color ❑ B/W		Consider size and stability of paper
Page 1: order of service			❑ Color ❑ B/W		
Page 2			❑ Color ❑ B/W		
Page 3			❑ Color ❑ B/W		
Page 4			❑ Color ❑ B/W		
Quotes and Scripture			❑ Color ❑ B/W		Consider which Bible version, written out or just referenced
My page "In memory of" facts about me, details specific to me			❑ Color ❑ B/W		
Prayers			❑ Color ❑ B/W		

C-7: My Funeral Program, *continued*

Updated on_____

Page	Graphics or Photos	Words *Note Preferred Font*	Color or B/W	Thoughts and Reasons	Other
Meditations			❏ Color ❏ B/W		
Songs All verses or just some			❏ Color ❏ B/W		
At the cross			❏ Color ❏ B/W		
Last page			❏ Color ❏ B/W		
Thanks and *appreciation* *of support*			❏ Color ❏ B/W		
Other			❏ Color ❏ B/W		

C-8: The Meal of Consolation

Updated on_____

The foods I love	Please serve as the meal of consolation	Why I like this food, special memories with it...	Don't you dare serve...	Other
Appetizers				
Entrees				
Salads				

The foods I love	Please serve as the meal of consolation	Why I like this food, special memories with it…	Don't you dare serve…	Other
Sandwiches				
Beverages				
Desserts				
Comfort foods				
Other				Rituals and/or traditions ❏ coffee and tea served ❏ videotape guests with a word for my family ❏ open mike for sharing goodbye stories ❏ other

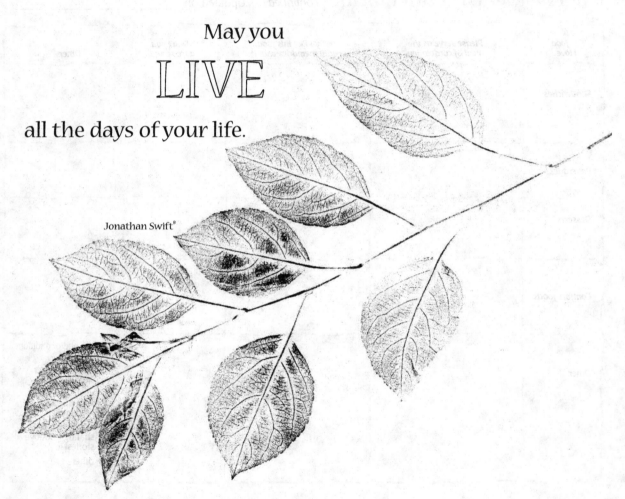

May you

LIVE

all the days of your life.

Jonathan Swift[8]

Final Preplanning Tasks

To be completed as I plan throughout the year,
or as I enter the thirteenth month of planning.

- ❑ Meet with the person(s) I have chosen to officiate at my goodbye party service. Give this person a copy of my plans and inform him/her of the location of my plans.

- ❑ Meet with the person(s) I have assigned as "Designated Person to help with final details." Give this person a copy of my plans and inform him/her of the location of my plans.

- ❑ Visit and interview the cemetery(s) I am considering. Visit more than one.

- ❑ Visit and interview the funeral home(s) I am considering. Visit more than one.

- ❑ Begin prepaying for the property at the cemetery.

- ❑ Begin prepaying all of the funeral expenses at the funeral home.

- ❑ Purchase an urn or casket.

- ❑ Purchase a register book (guest book) for the service.

_____

_____

_____

_____

_____

Maintaining My Goodbye Party Plans

Review YEARLY on:

- ❑ My Birthday

- ❑ New Year's Day

- ❑ Easter

- ❑ During Lent

- ❑ Memorial Day

- ❑ At the first funeral of the year

- ❑ On Retreat: scheduled for _____ (date)

- ❑ Tax Day: April 15 or _____

- ❑ Other _____

Review/Update every FIVE YEARS:

Next full update due in _____ (month) of 20__

Notes

Use these pages to write miscellaneous notes to yourself or to your family or designated planner.

Notes about what you like or don't like. Notes about what you are considering.

Notes about anything that does not fit into a workbook form.

Staple or tape items onto these pages. Draw on these pages.

Date your entries so that you and your planner will know how recent the entry is.

Notes

Use these pages to write miscellaneous notes to yourself or to your family or designated planner.

Notes about what you like or don't like. Notes about what you are considering.

Notes about anything that does not fit into a workbook form.

Staple or tape items onto these pages. Draw on these pages.

Date your entries so that you and your planner will know how recent the entry is.

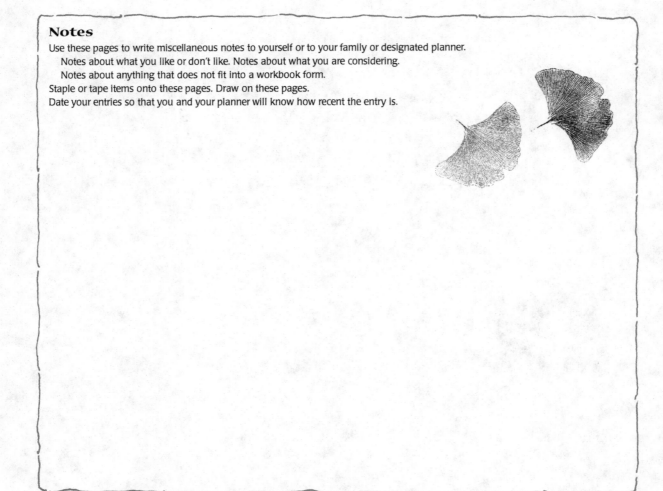

Yesterday is history, tomorrow is a mystery…today is a gift…

Eleanor Roosevelt[9]

Endnotes

[1]Kim C. Rice, *The Goodbye Party* (Victoria, B.C.: Trafford, © 2005).

[2]Sara Groves, "Going Home", *Conversations* (Sara Groves Music/admin. by Music Services, © 1999), compact disc. All rights reserved. Used by permission.

[3]Ted Loder, "I Teeter on the Brink of Endings," *Guerrillas of Grace: Prayers for the Battle* (Philadelphia: Innisfree Press, Inc., © 1984), p. 77. Used by permission.

[4]Jeremiah Gamble, "Sing Along Song (A Happy Reminder)," *Pour* an album by Poor Baker's Dozen (Minneapolis: Spirit Jockey Music/Sound Wagon Records, © 1998), compact disc. Used by permission.

[5]Maureen Pranghofer and Dan Adler, "Come To Me," *Some Run the Race* (Minneapolis, MN: Maureen's Music, © 1994), compact disc. Used by permission.

[6]Andrae Crouch, "Soon and Very Soon," *Living the Gospel* (Bud-John Songs Inc./Crouch Music Corp. ASCAP. © 1976 Lexicon Music, Inc. Under license from Platinum Entertainment, Inc.), compact disc. All rights reserved. Used by permission.

[7]Elias Porter, (1770–1840), http://www.smedg.org.au/riddell0803.html (accessed 07-02-04).

[8]Jonathan Swift, (1667–1745), http://www.online-literature.com/quotes/quotation_search.php?author=Jonathan%20Swift (accessed 07-02-04).

[9]Eleanor Roosevelt, (1884–1962), http://www.motivational-inspirational-corner.com/getquote.html?authorid=31 (accessed 07-02-04).

[10]Sara Groves, "Going Home," *Conversations* (Sara Groves Music/admin. by Music Services, © 1999), compact disc. All rights reserved. Used by permission.

I've been feeling kind of restless. I've been feeling out of place.
I can hear a distant singing,
a song that I can't write, but it echoes in what I'm always trying to say.

There's a feeling I can't capture.
It's always just a prayer away.
I want to know the ending, things hoped for but not seen,
but I guess that's the point in hoping anyway.

Going home, I'll meet you at the table.
Going home, I'll meet you in the air.
You are never too young to think about it.
Oh, I cannot wait to be home.

I'm confined by my senses, to really know what you are like.
You are more than I can fathom, more than I can guess,
and more than I can see with human sight.

**But I have felt you with my spirit.
I have felt you fill this room.**
This is just an invitation, a sample of the whole,
and I cannot wait to be going home.

Going home, I'll meet you at the table.
Going home, I'll meet you in the air.
You are never too young to think about it.
**Oh, I cannot wait
to be home.**

Face to face how can it be?

Face to face how can it be?
Face to face how can it be?

Sara Groves[10]

Order more books today!

Please send the following information along with your check or money order to:

The Goodbye Party Consulting Group

P.O. Box 331

Hamel, MN 55340

Name: _____

Address:_____

_____

City: _____

State: _____

Zip: _____

Phone: _____

Fax: _____

E-mail: _____

Books	Cost	S and H	Total (Non-MN residents)	MN Total (6.5% tax added)
One	$29.95	$6.50	$36.45	$38.81
Two	$59.90	$9.25	$69.15	$73.64
Three	$89.85	$9.25	$99.10	$105.54
Four	$119.80	$13.00	$132.80	$141.43
Five	$149.75	$13.00	$162.75	$173.33
Six	$179.70	$13.00	$192.70	$205.23
Seven	$209.65	$0.00	$209.65	$223.28
Eight	$239.60	$0.00	$239.60	$255.17
Nine	$269.55	$0.00	$269.55	$287.07
Ten	$299.50	$0.00	$299.50	$318.97

Please allow three weeks for delivery.

Questions? Want to order more than ten books?
Call 763-464-1185 or e-mail store@goodbyeparty.com

To pay by credit card please order from the website:
www.goodbyeparty.com

Visit

www.goodbyeparty.com

for our full product catalog.

Printed in the United States
By Bookmasters